Instant jQuery Masonry How-to

Utilize the power of Masonry in short, easy-to-follow recipes

Kyle Taylor

BIRMINGHAM - MUMBAI

Instant jQuery Masonry How-to

First published: May 2013

Production Reference: 1170513

Published by Packt Publishing Ltd.
Livery Place
35 Livery Street
Birmingham B3 2PB, UK..

ISBN 978-1-78216-502-6

www.packtpub.com

Credits

Author
Kyle Taylor

Reviewer
Ioannis Chatzikonstantinou

Acquisition Editor
Martin Bell

Commissioning Editor
Poonam Jain

Technical Editors
Dennis John

Ishita Malhi

Copy Editors
Aditya Nair

Laxmi Subramanian

Project Coordinator
Suraj Bist

Proofreader
Aaron Nash

Production Coordinator
Prachali Bhiwandkar

Cover Work
Prachali Bhiwandkar

Cover Image
Conidon Miranda

About the Author

Kyle Taylor is a 2012 graduate from the University of North Texas with a Bachelor of Arts in Information Technology, with a focus on network security. While in school, he and his colleague, Brett McCormick, published their paper on Public Transportation Tracking System Powered by Mobile Phones from the American Public Transportation Association.

He is also currently a Startup Weekend organizer and StartupDigest curator in the North Texas area and is very passionate about the Startup community. He is currently working with an organization that promotes open data and civic engagement in the city of Dallas.

When he's not working on startup projects, organizing hackathons, or networking with other entrepreneurs at meet ups, he enjoys being a frontend developer while dipping into mobile development whenever he can.

Currently, Kyle works as a Drupal developer for LevelTen Interactive in Dallas, Texas.

I would like to thank my fiancée, Maggie, for encouraging me to take every great opportunity possible, as well as my family and friends who have supported me along the way.

About the Reviewer

Ioannis Chatzikonstantinou is a lecturer at the faculty of Architecture, Yaşar University, Izmir, Turkey.

Currently he is pursuing his PhD at the Chair of Design Informatics of TU Delft, on Computational Comprehension for Architectural Design Engineering.

He also completed his MSc in Building Technology from TU Delft in 2011, receiving the distinction of the best graduate of the Building Technology department for the academic year 2011-2012. He worked on a Thesis focusing on Evolutionary Computation for Airport Terminal Design.

He graduated as an Architect from the Aristotle University of Thessaloniki, Greece in 2006.

His research interests include Computational Intelligence and Applications in Design, Advanced Layout methods, Intelligent Interface Design, and Machine Learning for Design Tasks.

www.PacktPub.com

Support files, eBooks, discount offers and more

You might want to visit www.PacktPub.com for support files and downloads related to your book.

Did you know that Packt offers eBook versions of every book published, with PDF and ePub files available? You can upgrade to the eBook version at www.PacktPub.com and as a print book customer, you are entitled to a discount on the eBook copy. Get in touch with us at service@packtpub.com for more details.

At www.PacktPub.com, you can also read a collection of free technical articles, sign up for a range of free newsletters and receive exclusive discounts and offers on Packt books and eBooks.

http://PacktLib.PacktPub.com

Do you need instant solutions to your IT questions? PacktLib is Packt's online digital book library. Here, you can access, read and search across Packt's entire library of books.

Why Subscribe?

- ► Fully searchable across every book published by Packt
- ► Copy and paste, print and bookmark content
- ► On demand and accessible via web browser

Free Access for Packt account holders

If you have an account with Packt at www.PacktPub.com, you can use this to access PacktLib today and view nine entirely free books. Simply use your login credentials for immediate access.

Table of Contents

Preface

jQuery Masonry is a dynamic grid layout plugin. Masonry works by identifying the space needed by elements in a specific container on a web page and arranges them in an efficient manner that maximizes the use of the area given.

What this book covers

Setting up a single-width column system (Simple) shows you how to set up the very basic Masonry single-width column system around which Masonry revolves.

Setting up a multi-width column system (Simple) shows how Masonry allows us to define a set of multiple widths in CSS so elements can span across multiple columns.

Using Masonry with images (Intermediate) talks about how we can properly use images in conjunction with Masonry. Because Masonry depends on using the height and width of an element, we need to account for that.

Adding media for multi-width columns (Intermediate) shows how we can handle instances where we need to account for the addition of multiple types of media, such as videos and images; this is considering the fact that multi-width columns give a great look to blog rolls and news feeds.

Using fluid layouts (Intermediate) goes over how to set the column widths to use fluid layout instead of responsive layout when building sites for mobile interfaces.

Animating using jQuery (Intermediate) shows how we can have a little fun using animations, which comes shipped with Masonry, when resizing the container area.

Animating using CSS3 (Intermediate) goes over how we use CSS3 animations and Modernizr to help us fall back to jQuery.

Integrating with WordPress (Advanced) goes over how we can integrate Masonry with the popular WordPress CMS, owing to the rising popularity of using content management systems.

Integrating with Drupal (Advanced) goes over the modules and integration process of Masonry with Drupal, which is the next most popular used content management system.

Adding and reloading (Advanced) goes over using Masonry's append and reload methods to align newly added content into the existing grid. This recipe is helpful for situations where we work on specialized projects that might involve dynamically adding content to a web page.

Placing a corner stamp (Advanced) shows how to implement a corner stamp in our Masonry grid. This would be helpful because Masonry moves content around when the container has different widths, and sometimes we want to keep a specific element at the top at all times, such as an author bio or featured product.

Aligning items from right to left (Advanced) shows us how to use the built-in Right-To-Left support within Masonry because in some instances when using Middle Eastern or Hebrew languages, the text needs to be aligned from right to left.

What you need for this book

For this book, you will need a text editor or IDE, an up-to-date browser such as Google Chrome or Mozilla Firefox, and a copy of the jQuery Masonry plugin. We will be using a CDN in some cases, such as the base jQuery library.

Who this book is for

If you have a basic understanding of jQuery, HTML, and CSS3, this book is for you. It is recommended that you have some prior experience working with JavaScript and/or jQuery. If you are used to working with JavaScript and want to learn a new jQuery plugin that can add a beautiful, clean grid layout to your site, you will find this book a breeze to read.

Conventions

In this book, you will find a number of styles of text that distinguish between different kinds of information. Here are some examples of these styles, and an explanation of their meaning.

Code words in text are shown as follows: "Using jQuery, we select our Masonry container and use the `itemSelector` option to select the elements that will be affected by Masonry."

A block of code is set as follows:

```
<style>
  .masonry-item {
     background: #FFA500;
     direction: rtl;
     float: left;
     margin: 5px;
```

```
    padding: 5px;
    width: 130px;
  }
</style>
```

When we wish to draw your attention to a particular part of a code block, the relevant lines or items are set in bold:

```
<script>
  $(function() {
    $('#masonry-container').masonry({
      itemSelector: '.masonry-item',
      columnWidth : function(containerWidth) {
        return containerWidth / 4;
      }
    });
  });
</script>
```

> Warnings or important notes appear in a box like this.

> Tips and tricks appear like this.

Reader feedback

Feedback from our readers is always welcome. Let us know what you think about this book—what you liked or may have disliked. Reader feedback is important for us to develop titles that you really get the most out of.

To send us general feedback, simply send an e-mail to feedback@packtpub.com, and mention the book title via the subject of your message.

If there is a topic that you have expertise in and you are interested in either writing or contributing to a book, see our author guide on www.packtpub.com/authors.

Customer support

Now that you are the proud owner of a Packt book, we have a number of things to help you to get the most from your purchase.

Downloading the example code

You can download the example code files for all Packt books you have purchased from your account at `http://www.packtpub.com`. If you purchased this book elsewhere, you can visit `http://www.packtpub.com/support` and register to have the files e-mailed directly to you.

Errata

Although we have taken every care to ensure the accuracy of our content, mistakes do happen. If you find a mistake in one of our books—maybe a mistake in the text or the code—we would be grateful if you would report this to us. By doing so, you can save other readers from frustration and help us improve subsequent versions of this book. If you find any errata, please report them by visiting `http://www.packtpub.com/submit-errata`, selecting your book, clicking on the **errata submission form** link, and entering the details of your errata. Once your errata are verified, your submission will be accepted and the errata will be uploaded on our website, or added to any list of existing errata, under the Errata section of that title. Any existing errata can be viewed by selecting your title from `http://www.packtpub.com/support`.

Piracy

Piracy of copyright material on the Internet is an ongoing problem across all media. At Packt, we take the protection of our copyright and licenses very seriously. If you come across any illegal copies of our works, in any form, on the Internet, please provide us with the location address or website name immediately so that we can pursue a remedy.

Please contact us at `copyright@packtpub.com` with a link to the suspected pirated material.

We appreciate your help in protecting our authors, and our ability to bring you valuable content.

Questions

You can contact us at `questions@packtpub.com` if you are having a problem with any aspect of the book, and we will do our best to address it.

Instant jQuery Masonry How-to

Welcome to *Instant jQuery Masonry How-to*. The purpose of this book is to give you an instant understanding of how jQuery Masonry works and how to implement it in general scenarios.

Setting up a single-width column system (Simple)

In case you haven't already noticed, Masonry works by arranging elements in a grid-based structure. By using a grid, Masonry tiles will flow and get stacked in a very neat and organized manner, which will give us the brick-like appearance we want to achieve. In this section, we will learn how to set up Masonry, at the very minimum, for a single-column system.

Getting ready

To perform the steps listed in this recipe, we will need a text editor, a browser, and a copy of the Masonry plugin. Any text editor will do, but my browser of choice is Google Chrome, as the V8 JavaScript engine that ships with it generally performs better and supports CSS3 transitions (as you'll see later in the book), and as a result we see smoother animations when resizing the browser window. We need to make sure we have a copy of the most recent version of Masonry, which was Version 2.1.08 at the time of writing this book. This version is compatible with the most recent version of jQuery, which is Version 1.9.1. A production copy of Masonry can be found on the GitHub repository at the following address:

```
https://github.com/desandro/masonry/blob/master/jquery.masonry.min.js
```

For jQuery, we will be using a content delivery network (CDN) for ease of development. In the code bundle for this book, open the basic single-column HTML file to follow along.

How to do it...

1. Set up the styling for the `masonry-item` class with the proper width, padding, and margins. We want our items to have a total width of 200 pixels, including the padding and margins.

    ```
    <style>
      .masonry-item {
        background: #FFA500;
        float: left;
        margin: 5px;
        padding: 5px;
        width: 180px;
      }
    </style>
    ```

2. Set up the HTML structure on which you are going to use Masonry. At a minimum, we need a tagged Masonry container with the elements inside tagged as Masonry items.

    ```
    <div id='masonry-container'>
      <div class='masonry-item '>
      Maecenas faucibus mollis interdum.
      </div>
      <div class='masonry-item '>
        Maecenas faucibus mollis interdum. Donec sed odio dui. Nullam
    quis risus eget urna mollis ornare vel eu leo. Vestibulum id
    ligula porta felis euismod semper.
      </div>
      <div class='masonry-item '>
        Nullam quis risus eget urna mollis ornare vel eu leo. Cras
    justo odio, dapibus ac facilisis in, egestas eget quam. Aenean
    eu leo quam. Pellentesque ornare sem lacinia quam venenatis
    vestibulum.
      </div>
    </div>
    ```

3. All Masonry options need not be included, but it is recommended (by David DeSandro, the creator of Masonry) to set `itemSelector` for single-column usage. We will be setting this every time we use Masonry.

    ```
    <script>
      $(function() {
        $('#masonry-container').masonry({
          // options
          itemSelector : '.masonry-item',
        });
      });
    </script>
    ```

How it works...

Using jQuery, we select our Masonry container and use the `itemSelector` option to select the elements that will be affected by Masonry. The size of the columns will be determined by the CSS code.

Using the box model, we set our Masonry items to a width of 90 px (80-px wide, with a 5-px padding all around the item). The margin is our gutter between elements, which is also 5-px wide. With this setup, we can confirm that we have built the basic single-column grid system, with each column being 100-px wide. The end result should look like the following screenshot:

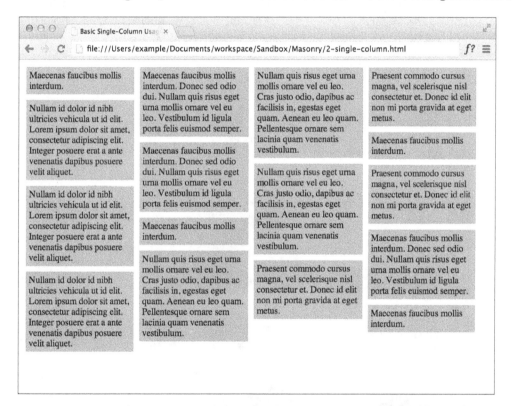

Setting up a multi-width column system (Simple)

Setting up a Masonry multi-width column instance is not that different from the procedure to set up a single-column instance. The main difference to know when using a multi-width column system is that elements can span across multiple columns; that is, we will have more than one column size defined in our CSS.

Getting ready

In the code bundle for this book, open the `2-Multicolumn.html` file in your preferred text editor to follow along.

How to do it...

1. Using CSS, we need to set up multiple classes for different column sizes. Every element's total width (which includes the padding and margins) needs to be evenly divisible by the column width we define in Masonry. If we have two elements of different sizes, such as 60-px and 100-px elements, we should choose our Masonry width to be 20 px. If we want the column width to be 100 px, all elements' widths need to be divisible by 100. Just to see the visual effect, let's render the columns in different colors, as follows:

```
<style>
  .masonry-item {
    margin: 5px;
    padding: 5px;
    float: left;
  }
  .column-1 {
    background: orange;
    width: 80px;
  }
  .column-2 {
    background: red;
    width: 180px;
  }
  .column-3 {
    background: green;
    width: 280px;
  }
</style>
```

2. The HTML structure is the same as a single-column structure, but we will now add the additional column classes that we created, to the Masonry items.

```
<div id='masonry-container'>
  <div class='masonry-item column-1'>
    Maecenas faucibus mollis interdum.
  </div>
  <div class='masonry-item column-3'>
    Maecenas faucibus mollis interdum.
  </div>
```

```
<div class='masonry-item column-2'>
  Nullam quis risus eget urna mollis.
</div>
</div>
```

3. The Masonry script is also the same as the single-column version, but we are going to add the `columnWidth` option and set it to `100`. Units are not required.

```
<script>
  $(function() {
    $('#masonry-container').masonry({
    // options
    itemSelector : '.masonry-item',
    columnWidth : 100
    });
  });
</script>
```

How it works...

Since we are being a little festive with the background colors, we can see that by setting a specific column width, the elements line up nicely across the defined columns (which you can see in the next screenshot). By setting multiple column classes, we can really mix it up and have fun with Masonry when we have lots of content.

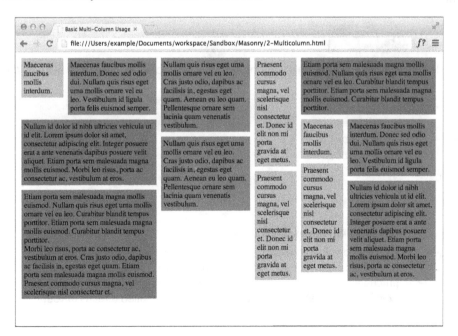

There's more...

In this example, we kept the size of the elements defined by the CSS divisible by the column width we set in Masonry. If you set the column width to a size that isn't a multiple of the base column width, Masonry becomes inefficient because there is wasted space between the column width defined in CSS and the column width defined in Masonry. You can play around with various widths to understand how it works, but this is why it is important to know how CSS and Masonry work together.

Using Masonry with images (Intermediate)

We often use images when building websites, so it's no surprise that we would like to use them in conjunction with Masonry. To avoid the common issue of the Masonry elements not aligning correctly when the dimensions of the images are not available when Masonry initially runs, we need to wait until the images have finished loading before applying Masonry. Luckily, Masonry comes shipped with a plugin called `imagesLoaded` for image support. We use `imagesLoaded` to wait for the images to finish loading, after which we need to let Masonry measure the images properly.

Getting ready

In the code bundle for this book, open the `3-images-loaded.html` file in your preferred text editor to follow along.

How to do it...

1. In this example, we are only working with images, so we only need to set our gutters in CSS.

```
<style>
  .masonry-item {
    margin: 5px;
    float: left;
  }
</style>
```

Downloading the example code

You can download the example code files for all Packt books you have purchased from your account at `http://www.packtpub.com`. If you purchased this book elsewhere, you can visit `http://www.packtpub.com/support` and register to have the files e-mailed directly to you.

2. We need to set up some images, so I'm going to use an image placeholder service called **LoremPixel**. This allows us to dynamically insert dummy images of whatever size and proportion we need. The images I will be using have three arguments after the base URL. The first argument is the width of the image, the second is the height of the image, and the third is the category of the image. The category is optional.

```html
<div id="masonry-container">
  <div class="masonry-item">
    <img src="http://lorempixel.com/250/250/technics" alt="random"
/>
  </div>
  <div class="masonry-item">
    <img src="http://lorempixel.com/250/350/technics" alt="random"
/>
  </div>
  <div class="masonry-item">
    <img src="http://lorempixel.com/250/450/technics" alt="random"
/>
  </div>
</div>
```

 The images used above are loaded in by an image placeholder service called LoremPixel (`http://www.lorempixel.com`). This allows us to insert test data without needing any actual files in our directory. All images used are licensed under the Creative Commons license (CC BY-SA).

3. To use `imagesLoaded`, we need to first wrap the Masonry container in a jQuery object, after which we can apply `imagesLoaded` and Masonry actions to the container object.

```html
<script>
  $container = $('#masonry-container');
  $container.imagesLoaded(function() {
    $container.masonry({
      itemSelector : '.masonry-item'
    });
  });
</script>
```

How it works...

The imagesLoaded plugin works by waiting until all the images have been loaded by the browser and then triggering Masonry. The result should look like the following screenshot:

If you do not use the imagesLoaded plugin, you will notice that the images load on top of each other in the same corner in the browser, as shown in the next screenshot. This is because Masonry was running before the images loaded completely, so it tries to organize a set of empty elements it doesn't know the size of. When imagesLoaded is used with Masonry, the script waits until all of the images have been loaded before triggering Masonry.

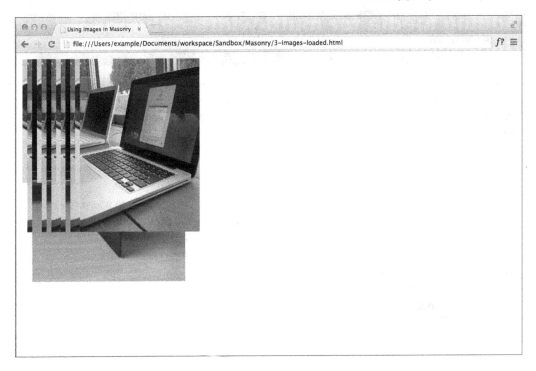

There's more...

There are some other alternatives to using the `imagesLoaded` plugin. For instance, we can assign each image a width and height property using the inline dimensions. Once these values are assigned to the elements, Masonry determines their spacing. Depending on how the site is being built, it might be tedious to ensure that all those image elements have height and width properties assigned.

The last alternative is to use `$(window).load()`. While this method isn't particularly efficient, as it can result in a potentially longer wait time, it does work; it waits until all the assets (such as images and media) are loaded into the window before triggering Masonry.

```
<script>
  $(window).load(function() {
    $('#masonry-container').masonry({
      itemSelector : '.masonry-item',
    });
  });
</script>
```

Adding media for multi-width columns (Intermediate)

Using Masonry with images and media is relatively simple, but it is not that straightforward when it comes to integrating media with multi-width columns. To implement integration with multiple widths, we need to look back at the multi-column technique and apply the same principles.

Getting ready

In the code bundle for this book, open the `3-images-loaded.html` file in your preferred text editor to follow along. There is a lot of additional styling used for various types of elements, so I will only be going over what directly affects the use of Masonry.

How to do it...

1. We only need to set the width of the various column classes we will be using with CSS.

```
<style>
  .masonry-item {
    background: #DEDEDE;
    border-radius: 5px;
    margin: 5px;
    padding: 10px;
    float: left;
  }
  .masonry-item img {
    display: block;
    height: auto;
    max-width: 100%;
    margin: 0 auto;
  }
  .column-1 {
    width: 170px;
  }
  .column-2 {
    width: 370px;
  }
  .column-3 {
    width: 570px;
  }
</style>
```

2. We will set up our HTML code with various types of media, such as images and videos.

```html
<div id='masonry-container'>
  <div class='masonry-item column-1'>
    <h3>Vehicula Vulputate Sem Ridiculus</h3>
    <p>Maecenas faucibus mollis interdum. Vehicula Vulputate Sem
Ridiculus</p>
  </div>
  <div class='masonry-item column-2'>
    <h3>Quam Ridiculus Vestibulum</h3>
    <div class="image-caption">
    <img src="http://lorempixel.com/400/300/technics" alt="random"
/>
    <span class="caption">Cum sociis natoque penatibus et magnis
dis parturient montes, nascetur ridiculus mus.</span>
    </div>
  </div>
  <div class='masonry-item column-2'>
    <blockquote>
    Porta sem malesuada magna mollis euismod. Nullam quis risus
eget urna mollis ornare vel eu leo. Curabitur blandit tempus
porttitor. Etiam porta sem malesuada magna mollis euismod. </span>
    </blockquote>
  </div>
  <div class='masonry-item column-1'>
    Praesent commodo cursus magna, vel scelerisque nisl
consectetur et. Donec id elit non mi porta gravida at eget metus.
  </div>
  <div class='masonry-item column-3'>
    <iframe src="http://player.vimeo.com/video/18743950"
width="560" height="320" frameborder="0" webkitAllowFullScreen
mozallowfullscreen allowFullScreen></iframe>
  </div>
</div>
```

The Masonry script in this exercise will use `imagesLoaded` in conjunction with the `columnWidth` option.

```javascript
<script>
  $container = $('#masonry-container');
  $container.imagesLoaded(function() {
    $container.masonry({
      itemSelector : '.masonry-item',
      columnWidth : 200
    });
  });
</script>
```

How it works...

Once again, we defined the `columnWidth` property and created a few CSS classes for the columns; inside the elements, we have various types of media, which were set using `imagesLoaded`. The result should look similar to the following screenshot:

Using fluid layouts (Intermediate)

When designing a site for a mobile interface, some designers prefer to use the fluid layout concept. This means that instead of assigning a fixed width to the columns, the width is set to a percentage of the size of the Masonry container. Assigning padding and margins correctly to the Masonry elements is similar to using fixed widths.

Getting ready

In the code bundle for this book, open the `3-fluid-layout.html` file in your preferred text editor to follow along.

How to do it...

1. Set the width of the Masonry elements to a particular percentage, and be sure to include the percentages of the padding and margins as well. For instance, if you want a four-column fluid layout, set the `width` property to `20%`, set `padding` (both left and right padding) to `1%`, and `margin` (both left and right margins) to `1%`, making the total width of the Masonry item 24 percent.

```
<style>
    .masonry-item {
        background: #FFA500;
        float: left;
        margin: 5px 1%;
        padding: 5px 1%;
        width: 20%;
    }
</style>
```

2. The HTML structure (shown in the following code snippet) is pretty standard, as in the previous recipes:

```
<div id='masonry-container'>
  <div class='masonry-item '>
    Maecenas faucibus mollis interdum.
  </div>
  <div class='masonry-item '>
    Maecenas faucibus mollis interdum. Donec sed odio dui.
  </div>
  <div class='masonry-item '>
    Nullam quis risus eget urna mollis ornare vel eu leo.
  </div>
```

3. To achieve a fluid layout, we will pass in a function for `columnWidth`. It is important to match this up with the width you set for the Masonry items. Setting the width to 24 percent suggests a four-column layout.

```
<script>
  $(function() {
    $('#masonry-container').masonry({
      itemSelector: '.masonry-item',
      columnWidth : function(containerWidth) {
        return containerWidth / 4;
      }
    });
  });
</script>
```

How it works...

In our CSS styles, we defined the width of the Masonry elements to be 24 percent of the container width [20% width + (x2) 1% margin + (x2) 1% padding]. In the highlighted part of the previous code snippet, we can see that we passed a function to change the width of the column to 25 percent (because the container width is considered to be 100 percent, and we divided it by four).

There's more...

Multi-columns can be implemented in a fluid layout as long as they are a factor of the fluid container width. For instance, if we have a four-column container, we can set the width of a two-column class to 46 percent with 1 percent each for margins and padding—a total width of 49 percent. Once we decide whether or not to go with a fluid layout, we need to be consistent when using percent versus pixels so as not to mix them up.

Animating using jQuery (Intermediate)

We have already noticed that Masonry is responsive while resizing the browser window and rearranges the elements according to the width of the container. By default, Masonry has built-in support for animation using standard jQuery animations.

Getting ready

In the code bundle for this book, open the `4-jquery-animation.html` file in your preferred text editor to follow along.

How to do it...

1. Start with the standard Masonry CSS code.

```
<style>
  .masonry-item {
    background: #FFA500;
    float: left;
    margin: 5px;
    padding: 5px;
    width: 80px;
  }
</style>
```

2. Build the standard Masonry HTML structure and add as many Masonry items as necessary.

```
<div id='masonry-container'>
  <div class='masonry-item '>
    Maecenas faucibus mollis interdum.
  </div>
  <div class='masonry-item '>
    Maecenas faucibus mollis interdum. Donec sed odio dui. Nullam
quis risus eget urna mollis ornare vel eu leo. Vestibulum id
ligula porta felis euismod semper.
  </div>
  <div class='masonry-item '>
    Nullam quis risus eget urna mollis ornare vel eu leo. Cras
justo odio, dapibus ac facilisis in, egestas eget quam. Aenean
eu leo quam. Pellentesque ornare sem lacinia quam venenatis
vestibulum.
  </div>
</div>
```

3. Add the standard Masonry script and then add the isAnimated option and set it to true.

```
<script>
  $(function() {
    $('#masonry-container').masonry({
      itemSelector : '.masonry-item',
      isAnimated: true
    });
  });
</script>
```

How it works...

By setting the isAnimated option to true, Masonry will automatically animate rearrangements using the built-in jQuery support. Now if we manipulate the width of the container by shrinking the browser window, we can see the animation in action.

The following screenshot was taken while the animation was happening:

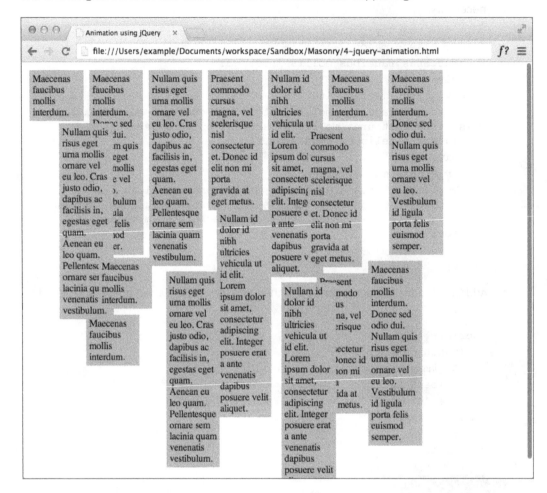

There's more...

We can include additional jQuery animation options using the `animationOptions` option. Some of the options include `duration`, `easing`, `queue`, `specialEasing`, `step`, and `complete`. Additional documentation for these options can be found in the jQuery documentation on the official jQuery website at `http://api.jquery.com/animate`. Some of these options can also be extended by using additional jQuery plugins.

```
<script>
  $(function() {
    $('#masonry-container').masonry({
      itemSelector : '.masonry-item',
      isAnimated: true,
```

```
        animationOptions: {
          duration: 500,
          easing: 'swing'
        }
      });
    });
  </script>
```

Animating using CSS (Intermediate)

As an alternative to animating using jQuery, we can use browser-supported CSS3 transitions. Using CSS3 transitions is beneficial in terms of performance because in some browsers and mobile devices, transitions are hardware-accelerated. The rendering engine of the browser can use frame skipping to keep performance smooth and also increase efficiency by reducing the update frequency of animations that are being used in hidden browser tabs.

Getting ready

In the code bundle for this book, open the `4-css-animation.html` file in your preferred text editor to follow along. Also, if you have not been using Google Chrome or a browser that supports CSS3 transitions until now, be sure to use one while performing the steps listed under this recipe.

How to do it...

1. Add the proper CSS3 transition properties in addition to the existing CSS properties that we have already defined for the Masonry elements.

```
<style>
  .masonry,
  .masonry .masonry-brick {
    -webkit-transition-duration: 0.5s;
    -moz-transition-duration: 0.5s;
    -ms-transition-duration: 0.5s;
    -o-transition-duration: 0.5s;
    transition-duration: 0.5s;
  }
  .masonry {
    -webkit-transition-property: height, width;
    -moz-transition-property: height, width;
    -ms-transition-property: height, width;
    -o-transition-property: height, width;
    transition-property: height, width;
  }
```

```css
.masonry .masonry-brick {
   -webkit-transition-property: left, right, top;
   -moz-transition-property: left, right, top;
   -ms-transition-property: left, right, top;
   -o-transition-property: left, right, top;
   transition-property: left, right, top;
}
</style>
```

2. Build the standard Masonry HTML structure and add as many Masonry items as necessary.

```html
<div id='masonry-container'>
  <div class='masonry-item '>
    Maecenas faucibus mollis interdum.
  </div>
  <div class='masonry-item '>
    Maecenas faucibus mollis interdum. Donec sed odio dui. Nullam
quis risus eget urna mollis ornare vel eu leo. Vestibulum id
ligula porta felis euismod semper.
  </div>
  <div class='masonry-item '>
    Nullam quis risus eget urna mollis ornare vel eu leo. Cras
justo odio, dapibus ac facilisis in, egestas eget quam. Aenean
eu leo quam. Pellentesque ornare sem lacinia quam venenatis
vestibulum.
  </div>
</div>
```

3. Add the standard Masonry functions without the `isAnimated` option.

```html
<script>
   $(function() {
      $('#masonry-container').masonry({
         itemSelector : '.masonry-item',
      });
   });
</script>
```

How it works...

Instead of using jQuery, we assigned CSS3 transition properties to the Masonry elements. After Masonry is run, it assigns additional classes and inline styles to the elements; for example, it assigns the `masonry` class to the container and the `masonry-brick` class to the individual items.

We assigned the `transition-duration` property to all items, the container itself and the Masonry items inside it, so that all transitions will last for half of a second. We then assigned the height and width of the container and the left / right / top positions to `transition-property`. This means that whenever those values change, that is, the size of the container and the position of the Masonry items change, the transition effect will be applied to those changes.

There's more...

Using CSS3 animations is great—they're efficient and they boost performance if the browser supports them. Luckily, if the browser doesn't support CSS3, we can use **Modernizr** and go back to using jQuery. Modernizr is a JavaScript library that detects the HTML5 and CSS3 features that are available in a user's browser, which is a great advantage.

 Modernizr is available for downloading at `http://modernizr.com/download/`. You can build your own custom Modernizr tests, such as adding CSS animations and transitions. Modernizr is available for free under the MIT license.

To enable Modernizr, we will have to include the Modernizr script into our page and then add the `isAnimated` option to the Masonry script with the value `!Modernizr.csstransitions`, as shown in the following code snippet:

```
<script src="js/modernizr.csstrans.js"></script>
<script>
  $(function() {
    $('#masonry-container').masonry({
      itemSelector : '.masonry-item',
      isAnimated: !Modernizr.csstransitions
    });
  });
</script>
```

This will detect whether CSS transitions are available in our browser; if not, we will go back to using jQuery animations. In the browser, we can view information about the DOM to see whether the CSS transitions and animations are enabled. In the following screenshot, we can see that CSS transitions are enabled in Firebug for Firefox:

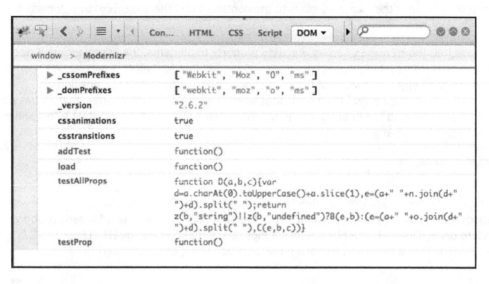

As opposed to that, in the following screenshot we can see that CSS transitions are turned off in Internet Explorer 9; we need to use jQuery to enable transitions:

```
Console    Watch    Locals    Call stack    Breakpoints
>> window.Modernizr
    {
        csstransitions : false,
        crosswindowmessaging : undefined,
        historymanagement : undefined,
        addTest : function(a,b){a=a.toLowerCase();if(!e[a]){b=!!b(),g.className+=" "+
        _enableHTML5 : true,
        _version : "1.7"
    }
    Add to watch



    ◄ [                          III                          ] ►

>> |                                                        ► ⌃
```

Integrating with WordPress (Advanced)

With the growing popularity of content management systems (CMS), integrating new features can sometimes be difficult. Even though there are some custom plugins available for integrating Masonry with WordPress, it is not necessarily as simple as that. To implement Masonry, we will need to edit a few theme files and use some functions to import our scripts. The upcoming recipe is somewhat complex, so if you don't get it the first time, don't worry! There is also more than one way to do this; if you work with WordPress often, build your site in a way that you are used to.

Getting ready

We will need an installation of WordPress, either local or on a server. In this demonstration, we will be using the version of WordPress that was most recent at the time of writing (WordPress 3.6) and modifying the **Twenty Thirteen** theme. Demo content has already been added, including categories, so we will be targeting the content of a specific category to apply Masonry to. The demo content being used in this example can be found under WordPress's theme-unit-testing page, located at the following URL:

```
http://codex.wordpress.org/Theme_Unit_Test
```

How to do it...

1. Open `content.php` in either the WordPress editor under **Appearance** or locally in a text editor, and locate the following line:

   ```
   <article id="post-<?php the_ID(); ?>" <?php post_class(); ?>>
   ```

2. Replace the line with the following:

   ```
   <article id="post-<?php the_ID(); ?>" <?php if ( in_category('9')
   && is_category('9')){ post_class('masonry-item'); }else{ post_
   class();} ?>>
   ```

3. In the same manner, open `category.php` and locate the following line:

   ```
   <div id="content" class="site-content" role="main">
   ```

4. Replace the line with the following:

   ```
   <div id="content" <?php if( is_category('9')){ print
   'class="masonry-container site-content"'; } else { print 'class =
   "site-content"';}  ?> role="main">
   ```

5. In the same `category.php` file, directly below the previous line is an `if` statement (`<?php if ( have_posts() ) : ?>`), and directly below that is a `header` section. Move the entire `header` section above the `site-content` area and below the primary area, and wrap it in the same `if` statement. When finished, it should look like the following:

```
<div id="primary" class="content-area">
    <?php if ( have_posts() ) : ?>
        <header class="archive-header">
            <h1 class="archive-title"><?php printf( __( 'Category
Archives: %s', 'twentythirteen' ), single_cat_title( '', false )
); ?></h1>
            <?php if ( category_description() ) : // Show an
optional category description ?>
            <div class="archive-meta"><?php echo category_
description(); ?></div>
            <?php endif; ?>
        </header><!-- .archive-header -->
    <?php endif; ?>
        <div id="content" <?php if( is_category('9')){ print
'class="masonry-container site-content"'; } else { print 'class =
"site-content"';}  ?> role="main">
        <?php if ( have_posts() ) : ?>
            <?php /* The loop */ ?>
            <?php while ( have_posts() ) : the_post(); ?>
                <?php get_template_part( 'content', get_post_format()
); ?>
            <?php endwhile; ?>
            <?php twentythirteen_paging_nav(); ?>
        <?php else : ?>
            <?php get_template_part( 'content', 'none' ); ?>
        <?php endif; ?>
        </div><!-- #content -->
    </div><!-- #primary -->
```

6. In the Twenty Thirteen theme folder, create a new JavaScript file named `custom-masonry.js` inside the `js` directory. Insert the following code into `custom-masonry.js`:

```
(function($) {
    var $container = $('.masonry-container');
    $container.imagesLoaded(function() {
        $container.masonry({
```

```
            itemSelector : '.masonry-item',
            isAnimated : true
        });
    });
}) (jQuery);
```

7. Open `functions.php` and add the following at the very bottom:

```
/**
 * Custom script for loading masonry when needed.
 */
function load_masonry() {
    if (is_category('9')) {
        wp_enqueue_script('custom-masonry', get_stylesheet_
directory_uri() . '/js/custom-masonry.js', array('jquery'), '1.0',
true);
    }
}
add_action('wp_enqueue_scripts', 'load_masonry', 20);
```

8. Lastly, we need to add our Masonry styles at the bottom of the `style.css` file:

```
.masonry-item {
    float: left;
    margin: 5px;
    padding: 5px;
    width: 380px;
}
```

How it works...

We did multiple things in this recipe, in the simplest way. To start with, we created a lot of demo content within the same category with an ID of 9. In `content.php`, we added the `masonry-item` class to each article if it was tagged in category 9 and if the current page had articles listed from that category. We did this by passing the class name into `post_class()`, which adds the `masonry-item` class to any existing classes that are applied to that article.

In `category.php`, we did pretty much the same thing. We added the `masonry-container` class to the content element, where posts appear if the category archive page is based on category 9. We also moved the header outside of the content area since it is not part of implementing Masonry and would break our page. Now we have a container and items we can apply Masonry to.

We created a JavaScript file that contains our Masonry script and we included the script by using WordPress's `wp_enqueue_script()` function, directing the source to the JavaScript folder in the theme; we then placed it in the footer with the other scripts by setting the last parameter set to `true`. To ensure that we are not running Masonry on every page, we put in another check to only load Masonry when on the category 9 archive page. When using the `add_action()` function, we set the last parameter to `20` to ensure that it loads after jQuery and that the core of Masonry has been loaded. After everything is completed, the result should look like the following screenshot:

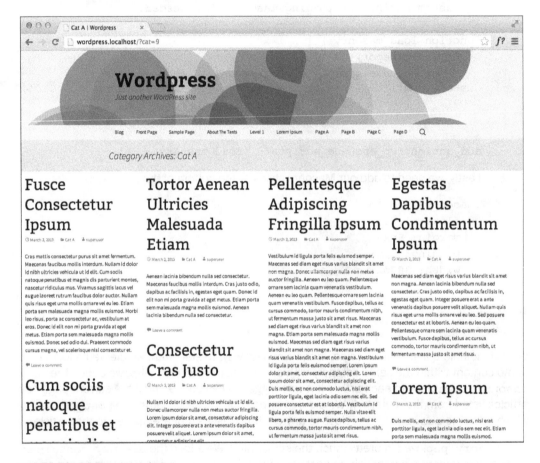

There's more...

We didn't need to load jQuery or Masonry because both are built into WordPress, making it really nice and easy. If we did need to, in WordPress, we would use the same `wp_enqueue_script()` method that we used earlier.

Integrating with Drupal (Advanced)

Luckily, with Drupal, integrating Masonry is relatively painless and easy to do. With the help of a couple of contributed Drupal modules, we can have Masonry installed in no time without having to write a single line of custom code.

Getting ready

As with WordPress, we need a local or server installation of Drupal 7. At the time of writing this book, the version of Drupal used was Drupal 7.20, with the default **Bartik** theme. We need to download five modules: cTools, Libraries, jQuery Update, Masonry, and Views. We also need to download the Masonry plugin, and if we need demo content, we can download the Devel module. Once the modules are downloaded, place them in the /sites/all/modules directory.

> At the time of writing, the current versions of the modules were as follows:
> - cTools – 7.x-1.2
> - Libraries – 7.x-2.0
> - jQuery Update – 7.x-2.3
> - Masonry – 7.x-1.1
> - Views – 7.x-3.5

After downloading, we will enable all of these modules, including the submodules Views UI and Masonry Views, and set jQuery Update to Version 1.7. Libraries and Masonry directories will not have been created yet, so create a folder named libraries in /sites/all, and then create a folder named masonry inside /sites/all/libraries. We will put the Masonry plugin in the /sites/all/libraries/masonry directory. Also, create some demo articles using Devel if no other content is available.

How to do it...

1. We will start by creating a new view, located in the administration menu, by going to **Admin | Structure | Views**.
2. Click on **Add new view**.
3. Name it Masonry.
4. Set the entity to be shown to **Content** and set the type to **Article**, as shown in the following screenshot.

5. Leave all other settings as default.

6. In the **Format** section of the Views user interface, set the format to utilize grids and leave all the default options for now, as shown in the next screenshot. Click on **Apply (all displays)**.

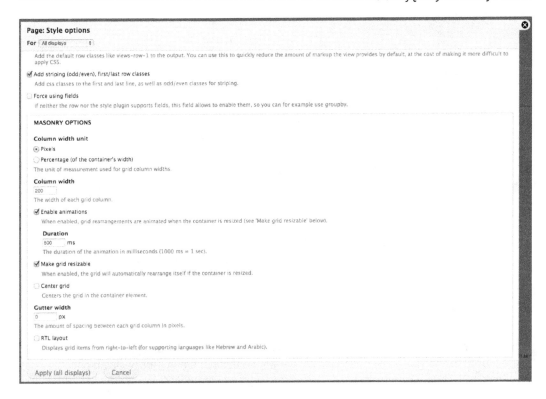

How it works...

The Masonry module is essentially a Views plugin with Masonry built in. Views is a query builder that posts content in a container based on the provided settings. This makes it easy to set up a page or view with Masonry while having the ability to change the settings through a GUI. If we go back and look at the Masonry grid settings, we can see that we can select or deselect Masonry options such as turning on animations and adding extra gutter space.

We needed the other modules as Masonry is dependent upon them. Most importantly, we needed `jQuery Update` to upgrade the core Drupal version of jQuery to a version compatible with Masonry.

There's more...

Using the default Bartik theme doesn't allow us to have a responsive mobile site. Switching our theme with a mobile-friendly version gives us the ability to enable animations and have a resizable grid. Some popular options include using the Bootstrap or Zurb Foundation's frameworks. To install, download Bootstrap from `http://www.drupal.org` and follow the instructions listed on the project page. Once the theme has been successfully enabled and set to default, we can watch Masonry animate while the browser window is resized.

Adding and reloading (Advanced)

When working on specialized projects, sometimes you need to build a feature that may involve adding additional content to a page, either through AJAX or through manual processes like comments and submissions. Fortunately for us, not only can we add new content to the Masonry container, we can also trigger Masonry to reload all the items to realign all Masonry elements back into a proper grid.

Getting ready

In the code bundle for this book, open the `5-add-reload.html` file in your preferred text editor to follow along. For this exercise, we will be using a small jQuery plugin called Placeholder.js to generate random text when adding new elements. Placeholder.js can be found at the following URL:

`https://github.com/decabear/placeholderjs/blob/master/placeholder.min.js`

 Placeholder.js is a lightweight, free jQuery plugin used to generate placeholder text (for example, "lorem ipsum") and placeholder images. Placeholder.js is freely available under the terms of the MIT License.

How to do it...

1. We will start off with the existing CSS properties that we have already defined for the Masonry elements. In this recipe, we will stick to single columns of width 150 px. Also, just for fun, let's make the dynamically generated items a different color for visual effect.

```
<style>
    .masonry-item {
        background: #FFA500;
        float: left;
        margin: 5px;
        padding: 5px;
```

```
      width: 130px;
   }
   .placeholder {
      background: #0BB5FF;
   }
</style>
```

2. Build the standard Masonry HTML structure; add as many Masonry items as necessary. We will also add a button above and outside the Masonry container because later in the recipe we will be dynamically generating additional Masonry items by clicking on it.

```
<div>
   <button id="add-html">Add HTML</button>
</div>
<div id='masonry-container'>
   <div class='masonry-item '>
      Maecenas faucibus mollis interdum.
   </div>
   <div class='masonry-item '>
      Maecenas faucibus mollis interdum. Donec sed odio dui.
Nullam quis risus eget urna mollis ornare vel eu leo. Vestibulum
id ligula porta felis euismod semper.
   </div>
   <div class='masonry-item '>
      Nullam quis risus eget urna mollis ornare vel eu leo. Cras
justo odio, dapibus ac facilisis in, egestas eget quam. Aenean
eu leo quam. Pellentesque ornare sem lacinia quam venenatis
vestibulum.
   </div>
</div>
```

3. Include Placeholder.js after Masonry, making sure to put in the correct relative path, and insert the following script:

```
<script src="js/placeholder.min.js"></script>
<script>
   $(function(){

      $container = $('#masonry-container');
      $container.masonry({
         itemSelector : '.masonry-item',
         isAnimated: true
      });

      //dynamically add Masonry items to the page
```

```
$('#add-html').click(function(){
    $add = $("<div/>", {"class": "masonry-item
placeholder"}).placeholder({"min": 15, "max": 50});
    $container.append($add).masonry('reload');
});
});
</script>
```

How it works...

For the first section, you can see that we're just running the ordinary Masonry script to set the Masonry items into the grid. We then assign a `click` event to the button we created and next bind an event handler that creates a new `<div>` class with the `masonry-item placeholder` class that get loaded with a random amount of text using Placeholder.js. Once the Masonry item is created, we use the jQuery `append` event to add the element to the end of the Masonry container; we then use the Masonry `append` method to apply the proper position to the appended item, which can be seen in the following screenshot:

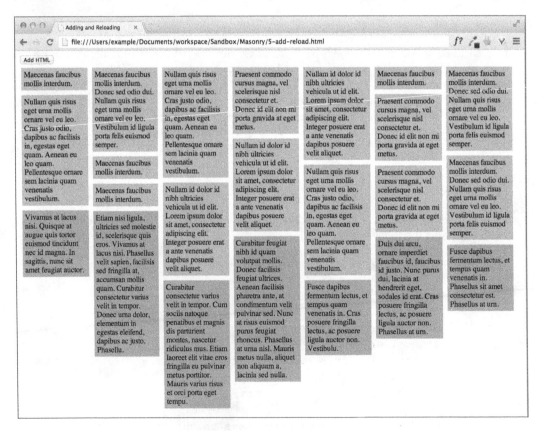

There's more...

Appending is great for adding content such as comments to the bottom of a page, but sometimes we need to add content to the top of the page. It is more than likely that this is a blog post or some other kind of time-sensitive material. We can easily switch the jQuery `append` method with the `prepend` method, which will insert our created content before all the other Masonry items. Note that we used the Masonry `append` method when appending an item (adding it to the end). If we use the jQuery `prepend` method instead of the Masonry `append` method, we need to use `reload`. This is because we don't know beforehand the size of the element that is being loaded in; so we reload all the elements to recalculate the alignment of the elements in the Masonry grid correctly. The result will look like the following screenshot:

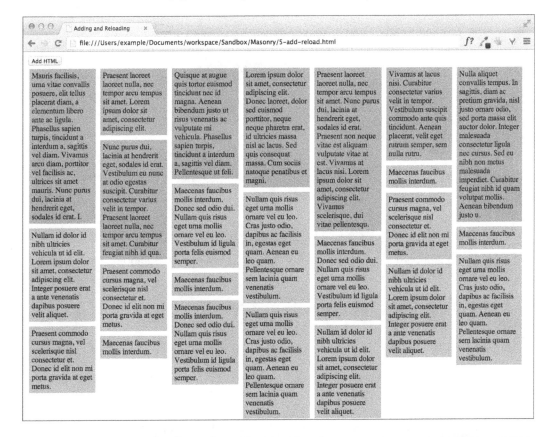

Placing a corner stamp (Advanced)

In Masonry, we can define a corner stamp, an element that will stay in the corner no matter where any of the other elements have moved. For example, a featured article in a list of blog posts or maybe a section about the author. Using the corner stamp is possible with a modification to Masonry.

Getting Ready

In the code bundle for this book, open the `3-cornerstamp.html` file in your preferred text editor to follow along.

How to do it...

1. Use the CSS properties that we have already defined in the *Setting up a single-width column system* recipe and make another class for the corner stamp.

```
<style>
    .masonry-item {
        background: #FFA500;
        float: left;
        margin: 5px;
        padding: 5px;
        width: 80px;
    }
    .cornerstamp {
        width: 180px;
        margin: 5px;
        padding: 5px;
        background: #DEDEDE;
        float: right;
    }
</style>
```

2. Add the standard Masonry HTML structure and then add an additional element with the `cornerstamp` class.

```
<div id='masonry-container'>
    <div class='cornerstamp'>
        Maecenas faucibus mollis interdum.
    </div>
    <div class='masonry-item '>
        Nullam quis risus eget urna mollis ornare vel eu leo.
    </div>
    <div class='masonry-item '>
        Praesent commodo cursus magna, vel scelerisque nisl
consectetur et. Donec id elit non mi porta gravida at eget metus.
    </div>
```

3. Before the Masonry script, add the following corner stamp modifications:

```
<script>
    // Masonry corner stamp modifications
    $.Mason.prototype.resize = function() {
        this._getColumns();
        this._reLayout();
    };
    $.Mason.prototype._reLayout = function(callback) {
        var freeCols = this.cols;
        if (this.options.cornerStampSelector) {
            var $cornerStamp = this.element.find(this.options.
cornerStampSelector), cornerStampX = $cornerStamp.offset().
left - (this.element.offset().left + this.offset.x +
parseInt($cornerStamp.css('marginLeft')) );
            freeCols = Math.floor(cornerStampX / this.columnWidth);
        }
        // reset columns
        var i = this.cols;
        this.colYs = [];
        while (i--) {
            this.colYs.push(this.offset.y);
        }
        for ( i = freeCols; i < this.cols; i++) {
            this.colYs[i] = this.offset.y + $cornerStamp.
outerHeight(true);
        }
        // apply layout logic to all bricks
        this.layout(this.$bricks, callback);
    };
```

4. Now add the standard Masonry script, with the `cornerstamp` class assigned to the `cornerStampSelector` option.

```
$(function() {
    $('#masonry-container').masonry({
        itemSelector : '.masonry-item',
        columnWidth : 100,
        cornerStampSelector : '.cornerstamp'
    });
});
</script>
```

How it works...

After specifying which element is the corner stamp, Masonry will keep the element in the corner while moving all other items around it. There are a couple of things that will break the corner stamp, which you need to take note of. The code for the corner stamp elements cannot have the class used to identify Masonry elements, in our case `masonry-item`, which is why we identify it separately. In this example, we put the corner stamp in the top-right corner by floating the element to the right, which can be seen in the following screenshot:

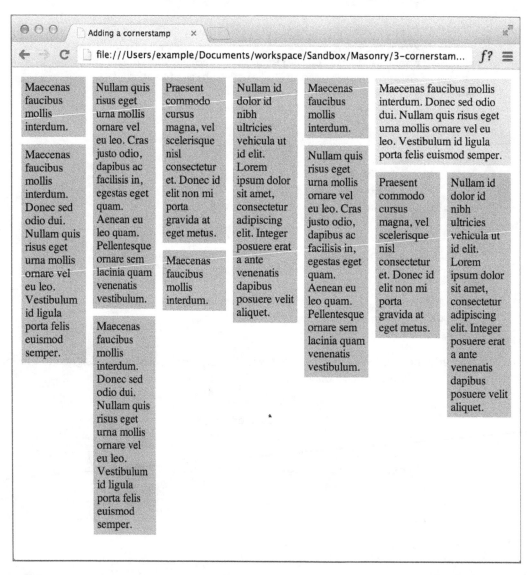

There's more...

If we want to put the corner stamp in the top-left corner, we can easily change the `float` property of the `cornerstamp` class from `right` to `left`.

Aligning items from right to left (Advanced)

For some Middle Eastern languages such as Hebrew and Arabic, script is primarily written from right to left. The W3C have written a standard that defines the text direction through attributes and CSS properties, but it is hard to make sense of these when the text direction is formatted from left to right. Masonry has a built-in option for such situations.

Getting ready

In the code bundle for this book, open the `5-rtl.html` file in your preferred text editor to follow along.

How to do it...

1. We will start off with the existing CSS properties that we have already defined for the Masonry elements. In this recipe, we have the choice of using either the `dir="rtl"` attribute on the Masonry container, or of defining the text direction in CSS. I think CSS is easier, so let us define it here.

```
<style>
    .masonry-item {
        background: #FFA500;
        direction: rtl;
        float: left;
        margin: 5px;
        padding: 5px;
        width: 130px;
    }
</style>
```

2. Build the standard Masonry HTML structure and add as many Masonry items as necessary.

```
<div>
    <button id="add-html">Add HTML</button>
</div>
<div id='masonry-container'>
    <div class='masonry-item '>
        Maecenas faucibus mollis interdum.
    </div>
</div>
```

```
<div class='masonry-item '>
    Maecenas faucibus mollis interdum. Donec sed odio dui.
Nullam quis risus eget urna mollis ornare vel eu leo. Vestibulum
id ligula porta felis euismod semper.
</div>
    <div class='masonry-item '>
    Nullam quis risus eget urna mollis ornare vel eu leo. Cras
justo odio, dapibus ac facilisis in, egestas eget quam. Aenean
eu leo quam. Pellentesque ornare sem lacinia quam venenatis
vestibulum.
    </div>
</div>
```

3. Using the standard Masonry methods, insert the following script; make sure to set the `isRTL` option to `true`:

```
<script>
    $(function(){

        $('#masonry-container').masonry({
            itemSelector : '.masonry-item',
            isRTL: true
        });

    });
</script>
```

How it works...

This is a fairly simple process. By default, when Masonry is setting the positions of items in the layout, it always starts from the left. For example, the inline style will look like this: `style="position: absolute; top: 0px; left: 300px;"`. When `isRTL` is set to `true`, the positioning starts from the right instead. This is a very simple technique, yet very effective. The result should look like the following screenshot:

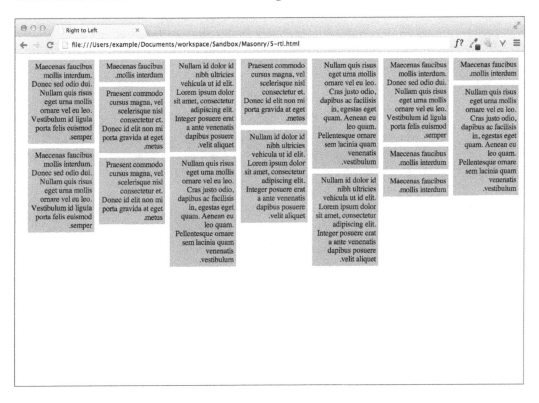

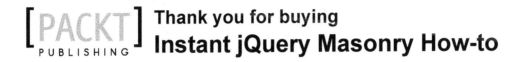

Thank you for buying
Instant jQuery Masonry How-to

About Packt Publishing

Packt, pronounced 'packed', published its first book "*Mastering phpMyAdmin for Effective MySQL Management*" in April 2004 and subsequently continued to specialize in publishing highly focused books on specific technologies and solutions.

Our books and publications share the experiences of your fellow IT professionals in adapting and customizing today's systems, applications, and frameworks. Our solution based books give you the knowledge and power to customize the software and technologies you're using to get the job done. Packt books are more specific and less general than the IT books you have seen in the past. Our unique business model allows us to bring you more focused information, giving you more of what you need to know, and less of what you don't.

Packt is a modern, yet unique publishing company, which focuses on producing quality, cutting-edge books for communities of developers, administrators, and newbies alike. For more information, please visit our website: www.packtpub.com.

Writing for Packt

We welcome all inquiries from people who are interested in authoring. Book proposals should be sent to author@packtpub.com. If your book idea is still at an early stage and you would like to discuss it first before writing a formal book proposal, contact us; one of our commissioning editors will get in touch with you.

We're not just looking for published authors; if you have strong technical skills but no writing experience, our experienced editors can help you develop a writing career, or simply get some additional reward for your expertise.

jQuery Mobile Web Development Essentials

ISBN: 978-1-84951-726-3   Paperback: 246 pages

Learn to use the touch-optimized, cross-device, cross-platform jQM web framework for smartphones and tablets

1. Create websites that work beautifully on a wide range of mobile devices with jQuery mobile

2. Learn to prepare your jQuery mobile project by learning through three sample applications

3. Packed with easy to follow examples and clear explanations of how to easily build mobile-optimized websites

jQuery for Designers: Beginner's Guide

ISBN: 978-1-84951-670-9   Paperback: 332 pages

An approachable introduction to web design in jQuery for non-programmers

1. Enhance the user experience of your site by adding useful jQuery features

2. Learn the basics of adding impressive jQuery effects and animations even if you've never written a line of JavaScript

3. Easy step-by-step approach shows you everything you need to know to get started improving your website with jQuery

Please check **www.PacktPub.com** for information on our titles

PUBLISHING

Responsive Web Design
with HTML5 and CSS3

Learn responsive design using HTML5 and CSS3 to adapt
websites to any browser or screen size

Ben Frain

PACKT

Responsive Web Design with HTML5 and CSS3

ISBN: 978-1-84969-318-9   Paperback: 324 pages

Learn responsive design using HTML5 and CSS3 to
adapt websites to any browser or screen size

1. Everything needed to code websites in HTML5
    and CSS3 that are responsive to every device or
    screen size

2. Learn the main new features of HTML5 and
    use CSS3's stunning new capabilities including
    animations, transitions and transformations

3. Real world examples show how to progressively
    enhance a responsive design while providing fall
    backs for older browsers

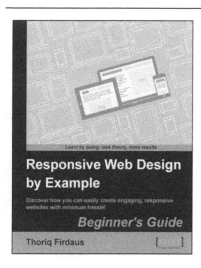

Learn by doing: less theory, more results

Responsive Web Design
by Example

Discover how you can easily create engaging, responsive
websites with minimum hassle!

Beginner's Guide

Thoriq Firdaus

Responsive Web Design by Example

ISBN: 978-1-84969-542-8   Paperback: 338 pages

Discover how you can easily create engaging, responsive
websites with minimum hassle!

1. Rapidly develop and prototype responsive
    websites by utilizing powerful open source
    frameworks

2. Focus less on the theory and more on results,
    with clear step-by-step instructions, previews, and
    examples to help you along the way

3. Learn how you can utilize three of the most
    powerful responsive frameworks available today:
    Bootstrap, Skeleton, and Zurb Foundation

Please check **www.PacktPub.com** for information on our titles